AF251990

1/2015
$12
.M21Q
OET

WINTER

Library of Congress Cataloging-in-Publications Data

Paultre, Eugénie, 1980-
        [Hiver. English]
        Winter / Eugénie Paultre ; translated from the French by
Cole Swensen, Etel Adnan and Simone Fattal.
                p. cm.
        ISBN 978-0-942996-83-8
        I. Swensen, Cole, 1955- II. Title.
        PQ2666. R37V7313 2009
        848'.91409-dc22

                                                        2008043572

copyright @ Editions Al Manar, 2014

@ The Post-Apollo Press for the U.S. edition, 2014

The Post-Apollo Press
35 Marie Street
Sausalito, California 94965

Book design and Cover photograph by Simone Fattal

Typeset by Alain Gorius
in Perpetua for the text
and Adobe Garamond Pro and Trajan for the titling

Printed in the United States of America on acid-free paper.

Eugénie Paultre

Winter

translated from the French
by
Cole Swensen, Etel Adnan and Simone Fattal

The Post-Apollo Press

For a while now I've been wanting to write to you – to
think out loud talk to you – in spite of all the daily obligations
overwhelming circumstances tenacious distractions – to feel
the discovery of the space around – immeasurable – a space
freely open to feel its dimension its just tension the necessary
abandon – to let thoughts gradually rediscover the alliance
and so I remember the time we spent together when the
winter made Paris so beautiful and there you were, so
assuring and tender when I could clearly see in the
December cold the defined contours of a possible life –
when around us was taking shape the order of a friendship
the beginning of intimacy – yes I've been wanting to write
to you for a while and the return of winter brings perhaps
with it the concentration needed to feel again this vital
benevolence
– a way of being – as you know so well to look around and
see the better self appear, and nowhere more than in the
details of daily life holding to the goodness of beings loving
its tremendous discretion its many manifestations the
promise of which it is the keeper

and maintain enough distance from the immediate to keep its
chaotic brutality from eating away at you — and thus be able
to welcome vivaciousness when it appears and also
to love the place that we have been given to inhabit it
beginning with our body and stretching throughout the
surrounding landscape stretching to the universe that
embraces us to love living in this space without wondering
why without questioning this space from which it's possible
to see the world with joy alone —
and yet — to follow a path — one's own — while being swept
along by the wake that precedes us that carries us drawn by
favorable works and actions — the innumerable enlivening
impressions — and so — under the cover of winter — of a
reserve — to see — perhaps — again — in it's own rhythm — an
attention — an aspiration — a gripping desire — the
inexhaustible gifts — and at the moment, I'm no longer afraid
of my presence to things — there are innumerable meanders
to acceptance — to go with it — to espouse movements in
their unpredictable directions in order to remain fluid
whatever the cost so that we don't break apart or shrink back
into repeated resignations — but to be alive to become more
and more alive trusting the fragility we're made of not
knowing why to be nourished by tenderness to stay sensitive
watchful to take the time whatever time it takes to
accompany the brotherly nuances of things as much as we
can — as you know so well

for a long time I've been wanting to write to you and this
new winter settling in slowly is more inviting
— a winter of impressions of disaster of vast confusion
holding even more closely and obscurely together — a "crisis"
they say a "crisis" — all around us week after week an ever-
amplified ever-activated echo —
this "crisis"— the key word impatiently tapping at every lip
anxious to make us feel its effects that becomes increasingly
obstinately haunting
a "crisis" for decades regularly repeated just to be forgotten
later to be repeated again, more troubling and insistent each
time
in a false voiceless cry crackling saying nothing but suggesting
arriving at a limit at a pain that doesn't know its own reach
— the result of an aging era charged with a false energy
apparently faltering

and then this — a cold dense exhaustion spreading fraying our
conscience even further a few more sufferings not making
themselves heard and the "revolutions" immediately
suppressed despite their lovely beginnings absorbed year in
and year out snatched away by globalized aggregation all
occurring with seemingly no discernment —

insidious consent?

it's winter
and we like to call it spring

but what can be done today to resist — something the heart
is inclined to do — to avoid giving in to the forced march
the unnamable tenacious cold to refuse to be seduced by the
current catastrophic renunciation

there's a great temptation to be here without being here to
reduce our roots in this earth to the senseless sufferings to
which it is said they're attached

— yes we carry the weight of a century of inhuman
pigheadedness angrily creating innumerable miseries —
dragging behind it a dense misshapen despair that spreads
out everywhere
and so many good minds decrypting analyzing explaining
trying contemporary enterprise to restate reassemble
structure
to synthesize
to progress
as if after shock
to wake up
to forget?

a shared void
this call
a disillusion
resolutely latent

with no counterpart
in indifferent agitation

(and so we are in an era of required entertainment and so
many centuries to get here the whole world a consumer
society dreaming of nightmares disastrous lies and we are so
many on earth what to think of all that   dispersion
abstraction which seems to put an end to the human
community the best for all — to be resigned to accept a
totalizing instead of a spreading actual anonymous
totalitarianism spreading all over an ungraspable 'meta-
empire" — not a spot on the globe will escape it not a spot
that could pretend to be a center in this world-universe
where multiplicity reigns where division spreads where unity
unities are made and unmade by a terrifying math —)

and yet right now
to be simultaneously nowhere and very much here
to not let oneself be constructed by fear

to try to identify to hold off the diverse machines that
amplify the thousand pains — watching and yet fearing to be
locked or be ceding to the seductions of powerlessness

whatever it is

to hold onto life with courage

to assess the present situation our situation to let oneself be
taken over by its effects its enormity

to feel the singular turn of our world from the inside despite
its confusion because of its particular confusion which won't
block anything as long as we can find in its natural suppleness
the space where to feel the climate rising all around

 and then
to put aside the pressing reasons
to measure in its own way
— personal —
the now
— to find oneself there —
there where we live —
that we have to forego
just to grow
— our now —
that preserves what's extraordinary
perceiving its truth
experiencing the truth
that cannot change
that loves to reveal itself then be concealed
in a thousand and one ways
like the sun

— and freely

to let yourself be carried away by the joy of the sea lit up by
its reflections by the marvel of all the skies in their
innumerable nuances the unavoidable flight of birds the
troubling immensity of the simplest gesture of affection the
depth of a face crossed by love

to believe in the good path of one's life no matter what life
to go along with its movement as dance marries music
anyone can do it to let go and follow ignoring what will
happen other than the possibility of our presence on this
earth

but there have been times so different from our own there
have been people countries nations kingdoms gods
today the world could disappear —
we're no longer amazed by such a possibility it seems a part
of us we who were raised with this idea an explosion not a
"deluge" as in times immemorial — the atomic bomb as an
unacceptable manifestation of an omnipresent reign of threat
— the always possible impossibility which makes the idea of
a final end familiar without our really knowing what it
would mean as our world seems for us to mean - everything
everything
it asks us to love it entirely and asks us to forget it and
asks us not to forget it — the world our world — at the mercy
of — because of us in spite of us? — the innately negative
complications of imbecilic games of power an obsession that

settles a little more each day a frenetic inventiveness a little
more each day the world suffers from a negligence a
negligent yet permanent destruction that favors the least of
our weaknesses?

what can be done?

— yes, what can be done?

at best
fight for yourself
accept to live
at a minimum level
within the bounds of a protected perimeter?

each one for himself?

each one for himself
yes
each one for himself

to keep to oneself

but to wonder

       within ourselves

about what we are

to honor our birth to watch over our death to eat to rest to
lean on the earth
with a child's trust
— to feel able
to love freely
as the living vibration communicates joy to joy
not to unlearn the joy that gives birth to joy
but meet whatever comes
to find recognize the warmth of the right feeling
to be happy simply that
the strength we have
heading into the unknown that knows why
there's a human pride that acts for us as a living breath
a maturity now the guardian of our secret named freedom
movement forgetfulness and music
maybe our slightest gestures have an astral meaning and no
other
the taste of water is sensational
can be sensed like the passing of a cloud between clouds
anything better than closing in upon oneself
the enthusiasm for life is striking
to live for that alone

— thinking about our era's disaster will get us nowhere but I
can't stop doing it and I miss the freedom to remember all
the moments of innocent joy that necessarily compose every
existence

the strength for life is found inside an arid solitude — to wait
so often for the strength for life to impose itself because
that's just how it is

I love summer and its intolerable suspension and we must
never forget its impulse to strip everything bare

no the world is not senseless why would it be and how and
who can say that it is no the world is not senseless so many
fully-lived moments remind us of this
to refuse to admit the absurd
it's dangerous to ask this question to become this question
"why" which immediately changes into a more dangerous
one which is "what for" after that there's nothing to hold on to

I see only one thing completely serious and that is joy the
sense of joy
has there ever been a god of joy?
"joy" the word is enough in itself to open a pure space —
eternally open a plain a hill then another then the sky —

— the West has spread all over the earth thus disappearing
today its history is ending is closing up upon us History has
taken place and only stories remain innumerable stories to be
told the West has given birth to fiction in a final jolt —leaving
truth to its scintillating unreal reality

— to feel that there's no choice and at times turn one's head
to escape for a minute then drown again to breathe again —
there's that moment when the mind is freed and can't be
touched by anything making room for that which can be fully
felt

we each live happily in beautifully broad parentheses — as if
protected by delicate boundaries that allow us to breathe

— I wish I'd never seen the sea to see the sea for the first time
— discover the world in its openness its impossible continuity

and not come back

right in front the light
confuses one's sight holds it loses it

the earth beneath our feet and the sky above us equally — the
freedom to find the right move — fraternity helps us become
fond of some of those around

equally freely fraternally
to embrace
our human condition
in the same revolution

given
shared

– "I exist"
there are so many mysteries presented like this
so many blinding mysteries

– "to love"
everything invites us
                    artfully
to give ourselves to immensity
to infinity
yes this is asked of us
for which we die

the inner way is the ultimate revolution
everyone is personally asked to return to himself
for good
we have to live up to the measure of our true abyss

keep calm in the face of it
to lose what you lean on

          just long enough to find it again more certainly

– blue on grey on blue on white in stages of tenderness
stained with an omniscient rose a touch of sky that suddenly
returns one's taste for life

to naturally spring back to the surface

– it's wonderful how life is ideally designed to be swept into
the game it's stronger   than we – we're all half children and
can't do a thing about it – it's stronger than we – to be happy
to be happy as little as that to feel levity

how simple it is to live as long as we live

it is so beautiful that we all spontaneously think that life is not
worthless it's so beautiful that mothers raise their children
it's so beautiful that we sleep at night so beautiful that there
are seasons rain stars a sky a sun seas continents and earth
that we can reach in the highest degree we end up looking a
little bit like them at times as imperceptibly as perfectly
shaded images an unintentional declination

– there are elemental colors elemental lines elemental words
elemental gestures nourished by what's elemental in order
to grow that's how everything gets to be raised to be fed on
blue and yellow and red let's finally be happy to live in the
universe and in its smallest details what your eyes inspire
what your words convey to me to feel deeply the
world/matter to love the essence of gratitude and from the
universe the world is born it's a path that we have to
complete – to love our neighbor as we love ourselves to find
the trust in things find the point where life from life springs
where the miracle works

— but what will become of us?
everything happens as though nothing were wrong we're not
asleep we're tired or drugged with an energy not ours it's
an order coming from afar but where from do we get the
faculty to live as if it were a race with no end just a vague idea
just sharp enough to let us put one foot in front of the other
going nowhere but fired by an unclear and obscure need
based on instinct even though we ourselves will be obliged
to live horizontally at our own height in a narrow space
choking and crowded with a fleeting futility and pale
depictions a space with few details
the high and the low — are they still as distant as they once
were — must be sought again in the simplest emotion but the
daily is so harrowing because it endlessly demands
submission again and another and another again

— must we be higher than things rise above them or be
beneath them all the way down — there's always the
temptation to gain a little distance as if you could find a way
out because you certainly can't stay as is — therefore we're
here and there therefore the need to adjust is constant the
sense of justice as natural as the necessary solitude that
ultimately makes us what we are at the end it's the best of
what's left for us — it's a tiring life made largely of little
things that require tremendous concentration unbelievable
energy but everyone does what they can to give form and
consistency to whatever comes along

to simply arrive at living

day after day

to see more clearly on certain days on others grey grey white
dark grey color again and again

with more resistance the predictable course of events would
be less sad less bland certain dreams would be less real than
the tangled impressions that make up the texture of the
staccato succession of these troubled days

— yes living is an effort it's strange it's revolting it's strange
that it's revolting — to be unable to act like it was easy to live
loving is I know a fantastic country a prodigious accident
the world is so vast and so small so multiple and so similar
strangely familiar ready to invade us like heavy rain making
the sky turn round in the sudden burst of its cadence —
seeing nowhere in this light but this sweet limit we hold onto
there is no assurance but the beauty of a heart beating so
lightly in its unlikely flight the calm we are what we are led
to an inside more inside than the inside still —

the dream of making this happen —

like music
— near and far —
placed on our lips

— ascending

— sunny-ing —
with insistent intensity —

— the sky and the sea are so thoroughly married that they
constitute a happiness nothing can ignore

 — yes you've frequently told me shown me that we each
create a morality with every move that we make — morality
as dance — and artists and their works would provide
successive clues on how to hang on to life the manifestations
of a character which has with constancy achieved the best of
itself with a vitality a good health that presume an art of
starting of stopping in time of continuing to insist on
avoiding the overly easy of mainly going for it alone — and
doing all this requires the invention of a very personal
discipline that can be grasped in a glance Rimbaud Mozart
Van Gogh as many admirable ways of living that are close
possible — a continuous secret effort

— there's a certain opacity that blurs our vision every
moment there's an agreement as transparent as the air we
breathe there is at once a resistance an understanding there
is in us an attraction a desire to unite with what is gathering
all around us

to follow this aspiration — courage love generosity all take
form in a singularly unexpected manner and belong to no
one in particular distributed through improvising human
beings —

isn't it essential to be aware of the light of the sun as it sows
its tenderness among the instants

— how good it is not to have to hide —

and if today was the end it won't be ours to know we're
allowed to see without seeing to hear without hearing a
breath as if we had to remember serenity it's based on almost
nothing submerged forgetting that we are alive
a light wind the curves of a mountain the flow of passing
people the lit up distance of a face an inexpressible gesture
they all can protect us for a moment from many errors
because this is how it is as at times it is difficult to live as in
spite of oneself without reason without noticing it to hold
the rhythm which comprehends us real courage ignores itself
but is the most natural way of being what we are

— the blue of the sky here's something solid on which to rest —

— how good it is for language to be all the magic that it
essentially is —

sleep overtakes us fitted to our limits to wait quietly for
something indescribable made of all of life in its marvelous
loving lovable limpidity a prism

lost glance distant glance shared strength clear assurance
feeling of truth memory of a music to love oneself just

enough to love to wake up to feel lightning as a necessary
link this will come to pass will be lost again it will take a long
time to find it again only to lose it again to agree with it as
long as there would be in our obscurity this spot that so many
human beings have looked for and found more or less
distinctly but nonetheless with each new generation it all has
to be started again with the feeling that it will never ever
end that the universe will never be able to end as long as
we're searching in its midst for its sovereign heart — eternity
is played again — an inexhaustible gift — one must come close
reasonably prudently to an enthusiasm that could pulverize
us we must know how to wait to be stirred to discover who
we are as far as it's given to us to find ourselves

— and fortunately there is color color that possesses us color
is sacred a human chemistry a divine gift color a joy its
experienced radiance is the manifest sign that we are alive it
tends to find naturally and from within a certain order it
indicates and confirms the absolute reality of the heart it's
also necessary to love to be seized by love to give the world
something to give back to it some of what it has given us this
impression of self-sufficiency of simply being there an effect
that surges up brief and clear

we live in color we're made of and it lives in us
immersed in color in continuity — natural element vital
element
color — a possibility to live

we're all involved solely and individually in the search for
such a possibility as the solution to a problem

— a knowledge held silently
that steals from meaninglessness the space that we own —
there's a certain kind of contented discontent whose
generosity is felt through work —
there's an unavoidable insecurity but we can find at rare
moments the meaning of a totality to which we belong

— now right now the time when edges faint away I learn
everyday and this will not end a balancing act between
thoughts events and people a great composition to be
repeated incessantly there is the inner life to discover there
is the stream of events and this has no end —

to love the encounter

and through spontaneous friendships implicitly encourage
the strength we all must deploy to live

— to live one must in one way or another be supported and
find in oneself what gives us that strength and guess which
signs make the real first chords of our existence

as the poet knows how to discover and invent in a language
the infinite variety of the vitality of everything able to assume
the entirety of life loving on the sole condition of love itself

when philosophy starts and stops at the precise point where
a way of thinking opens out that's free of any anxious closed
or preconceived categories complete thought required
passage for anyone who wants to learn how to disrupt the
kind of process – the logic – by which we're supposed to
function today--we must be able to walk calmly with a light
heart along the ways of thought willingly chosen – the state
of being alive the fact of being alive the art of finding the
right balance and stature would summarize the meaning of
all human endeavor – it doesn't mean to put it in order but
to be with it and lovingly stay there we are on the verge of
discovering reality in its profound beauty discovering the
moment where one can do nothing but see things as they are
no matter what they are we are drawn to a decisive
wandering that we must nourish –

– winter – calm serenity of the high mountains – their power
their nobility – to verify something in spite of yourself – the
light of the sky of the snow which eases the gaze while
sharpening it – eclipses color without awakening nostalgia
because it unfolds ad infinitum the desire to see – the snow
delicately placed on earth ardently underscores the
incredible destiny of what is dear to us – and the cold allied
with whiteness with sweetness – there must also be a reason
for that –

the world as it is all by itself love as the sole condition the
strength that it all takes the one available just what's needed

but so much else erased like a dream and reality often so
overwhelming and always so many choices but above all
we're the interval in which the tone of the day is decided
full sun cool air light breeze where am I if not in the
wonderful place that I would wish to last forever there is so
much to be lived to serve all that has been given to our care
to give life to what's still dormant to what's calling us —
we are so well-loved it's a grave error to ignore it but don't
worry it's enough to yield to the kindness that possesses us
the faces all around reveal so many possibilities when looked
at with proper attention — subtle and precise variations
sometimes make us change the soul too loves to come fully
into being thus the world is also always changing and always
itself — to go through the fluidity of things not letting bitter
tensions mix with pure emotions

— and there are so many beings whose existence we would
never suspect all those we pass every day on the street
different every day the same every day so many human beings
that we see without seeing and that we never see again to
love this necessary presence this humanity that has so many
faces it is extraordinary how much these people manage to
succeed trying courageously you can see it in the way they
walk   — it's as if though we don't know them they're
supporting us encouraging us with their constant presence
taking over from the trees from the sky creating new and
invigorating obligations

— but often — reasonably without reason? — to refuse to
tolerate life's rushing by as we're anxious to stop everything
exhausted by a stifling and impeding blackness — and yet
something remains the heartbreaking ability to be patient a
spontaneous presence — to hold on to succeed — all of love
resides in the intensification of the self — to look for tension
in its own texture — to agree with that because that's how
it is — to let time create the days one after the other
discovering perhaps a truth or sharpening the sense of their
succession coming and going with the hope of a brighter
clarity of the latter's velocity nothing happening for nothing
day after day exhaustion growing
to recover strength
to connect with the tempo of the melodies of events
eternity comes about in its own time
a loving attention
not to sever oneself from one's basic sensitivity
to let go
day after day
an incompressible rhythm

to get there stay there
inevitably
— to agree with it all
because that's how it is

wind in the trees grey sea soft sounds winter arriving
uncertain silence breath of the sky autumn colors breeze on
breeze cold outside fragile branches clouds on a background
of blue sky invisible blue distant men wise buildings

underground forces friendly presences cold hands lasting
instants first loves clutched fears tender-grey light
November –

I can no longer remember I can no longer forget I'd rather
listen to my breathing feel the presence of things around
follow my thoughts go with their vigor

to love in broad daylight

are we separated from each other by being each assigned a
consciousness that demands a mental space apparently walled
off implicitly separated from each other firmly separated
from the living as much as we are from the dead as if all our
effort consisted in finding ourselves and making the
connections that keep the world every second from
crumbling connections of a primordial love conceived the
very first day of the very first day felt with closed eyes – so
many hardships that are the results of a despair furiously not
finding its language – we live within a defined perimeter but
we exist in an infinite space – we can't love life to the point
of not bearing the idea of losing it and yet we love it so much
the love of life animates us so deeply –

to love the life that's not entirely us there are so many
pointless ways of thinking of death that death becomes
superfluous brutal vague it's still better not to think about it
thus following our natural inclination – in fact it's wonderful

to see how easily we forget that we are going to die it is not
cowardice or foolishness it's life we are alive and we are
mortal we are alive and we are at the same time not alive
participating in the luminous night — our memory

— a smile noticed received from the blue side of his tender
heart his voice always able to make the living nuance of his
face vibrate all the way across to me clear light so gently
shared sound of a breath a river balanced on the fate of our
attention always willing to be submerged warmth and
courage hold us
to touch the core of life
where the body comes to be
to get to the secret of our impulsion —
exhaustion takes us away and brings us back to ourselves
— to reach the self
as it is required from us as never before

— but today there's a battle that's been going on for a long
time between us as if unwillingly and a system a kind of a
totalitarian totalizing economy it's a trial with a possible
humanity at stake in which we all take part not just as
members of some camp made of a system or of the men who
resist it we belong no matter what to both camps we belong
to this war between humanity and non-humanity a war that
each and every one bears body and soul — unnamable
sufferings resulting from this confrontation all the conse-
quences that the artificial incorporation of this global economic

domination engenders our minds invaded colonized by the nameless subterranean thought that rules us that cannot be formulated although it is activated every second the process by which we have been requisitioned for so many centuries just to get to this point this terrifying alienation and this blind nihilism — or else — a way of discovering experiencing differently unfathomable resources? to think about it — well and without fear but with great love yes the great spontaneous total life-long love that cannot be taught to grow according to this measure the greatest love a human being is capable of

eternity belongs to us evanescent sound endless rhythm eternal insomnia darkness' dimension sky starry not to say impervious to promptitude as it is ours to know without knowing to follow inspiration with a strict abandon

— shining day dull night dream flavor scintillation smooth bodies memories radiant smiles white shadows amber light incandescence December —

— water as the closest thing to music immediately adheres to us uniting with every point of our consciousness and unconsciousness in perfect reunion

— love and movement are the same not to fear the beautiful sea sparkling white its flow its tenderness the gift is really a gift when it responds to the sensation of an imperious necessity

generosity a way of being swept away it's effortless as long as
it's a natural consequence a way of marrying the radiance
produced by the world in its entirety and continuously
there's a marvelous impression waiting for us — we live
within a certain rim of perception we wish it to be vast to
better get passionately lost to come and go among errors
accidents faults it's a necessary form of recognition and it's
good to stretch one's mind as far as possible to experience its
vigor

the singular sensation of sky visits any free spirit so that it
can hide in the tiniest corners of things the real is
recognizable in hardness as if matter were the way to the
world's density anonymous presence sweet protection this
tension that tends to be forgotten when it reaches constancy
this vitality that interferes slyly thanks to that thoroughness
the ability to gain position to feel deeply marriage's meaning
to agree to prolong justify amplify the desire to live and give
it substance and thus reach unknowingly a living secret

— life —
its mysterious and infinite face

and yes to pray to work to rest and pray to work to look at
a destiny from birth to death even though life unites with
movement from birth to death a labor sometimes more
sensitive accomplished unconsciously solitude is visited
equally by all that is our destiny we don't live for nothing we

know it intimately absolutely differently the waiting comes
upon us at last we are almost there

and up it starts again — we love anxiously reasonably we love
here's a native mobility whose face and form are sublimely
unpredictable to love in order to get lost

in order to not return to love more

yes

and in spite of myself I know with a knowledge I can't
explain that the world is good

it's the most contemporary thought I can have

perhaps because at the very moment when the world seems
fragile to the point of being ready to disappear a time of
catastrophic determined and forced negations real or ever
more immanent — it's necessary to love more than ever
the world as it has been given to live it suddenly brusquely
as if by absolute necessity as our love gives it body saves it yet
at the same moment at the same instant to know how to
renounce it renounce it forever leave it definitely — to
experience the world's intrinsic benevolence by continuing
to breathe I follow as much as I can the thread of my thoughts
turned inward and outward looking for nothing but a way
to feel the drive — faces bring so many possibilities when

looked at with sufficient attention and what could be more
joyful than finding this common point where to be together
– more than ever we love a happy ending the endless joy
that cannot end gifted with life's innocence given to each in
person it's our destiny – only personal – why does
consciousness exist as a gathering place we're not enclosed
in it but still it's the space where learning is made possible
and everything is in the search for the precise harmony the
one that sets the tone of the moment we will leave this life
a tonality which could be prolonged if I had to die tomorrow
I'd say fine life has already given me everything because it
taught me that life gives everything – I haven't always been
able to receive but it doesn't matter because I've learned it
in my own way – these endless days where love is
encountered – not to be lost again – without betraying its
mystery

mystery as a painting – something to be looked at leisurely
that doesn't die from being looked at for ever doesn't wear
out like do things we neglect – a painting is the proof of
existence's real dimension a proof that has to be repeated
with each era – no work no matter how close to eternity
would stand by itself everything starts again with each new
age

– we are often crossed by tensions that we have to dissolve
and transform into a verve entirely ours

to wipe off all shocks and counter-shocks
for the soul to reach light
to be prepared by love
thought again goes to sleep wakes up and then goes back to
sleep in series of brusque and brutal shifts and reshapings —
the astonishing alternation of a secret privilege
to find a place within the self

in oneself

— to return to the place where the world was given — a place
made of vigilant premonitions faithful amazements binding
friendships necessary concerns — forms colors sounds things
all alive in their own right and forming this palpable
connection to our being as a whole — thought ascends calmly
to the goodness to which it bears witness awakening the
immensity that sleeps within us so rich in promise that we
must create our own humanity whose essence is nourished
by the human beings past present and to come the human
community always already existing and each of us being able
to find within himself all that's needed to live to live humanly
the life of today which has become survival a spiritual
survival the soul unable to feed the ghostly shadows that
haunt us in a period in which we're all in one way or another
called to struggle for ourselves — to be then delivered to the
source of this deep hope and aspiration — to let oneself be led
to the self to find the place from where the marvel of
existing on earth can be felt

to meet there to join

to let unfold that perpetual drive whose trace we keep

to believe in the meaningful continuity of everything

— and see again and again
the blossoming
in its inevitable rebirth
its primordial fineness
to feel feel deeply
the familiar reason for its appearances
to aim for greater amplitude
to feel space in itself
love growing
within the beautiful trajectory it projects
to feel to reveal the real dimension of things
in their rhythm to be lost
sea sky mountains
sun moon
his gaze
and everything you love
— that which loves — yes —
over and over —
to cover the whole of time
according to its reason
for being

the miraculous night
its silence

By the Same Author

L'Etat actuel des choses, Editions Al Manar / Alain Gorius, Paris, 2012

Hiver, Editions Al Manar / Alain Gorius, Paris, 2013

Nous verrons bien, Ed. Moon Rainbow, 2013.
Illustration : six drawings by Etel Adnan.